SURVIVE!

SURVIVE!

Prepare for Tomorrow's Disasters Today

Ron Collins, MAed

iUniverse®

SURVIVE!
PREPARE FOR TOMORROW'S DISASTERS TODAY

The views expressed in this work are solely those of the author and do not necessarily reflect the views of the publisher, and the publisher hereby disclaims any responsibility for them.

iUniverse books may be ordered through booksellers or by contacting:

iUniverse
1663 Liberty Drive
Bloomington, IN 47403
www.iuniverse.com
1-800-Authors (1-800-288-4677)

Because of the dynamic nature of the Internet, any web addresses or links contained in this book may have changed since publication and may no longer be valid. The views expressed in this work are solely those of the author and do not necessarily reflect the views of the publisher, and the publisher hereby disclaims any responsibility for them.

Any people depicted in stock imagery provided by Getty Images are models, and such images are being used for illustrative purposes only. Certain stock imagery © Getty Images.

ISBN: 978-1-5320-8735-6 (sc)
ISBN: 978-1-5320-8736-3 (e)

Library of Congress Control Number: 2019917802

Print information available on the last page.

iUniverse rev. date: 10/30/2019

Contents

INTRODUCTION

Humans are intrinsically optimistic. We tend to see the most positive aspect of any activity regardless of the circumstances that surround us. As children, we imagine we are the hero of the game, hitting a grand slam in the bottom of the ninth; the princess who saves her kingdom from evil forces; or even the president who saves the world. However, as adults, we learn reality is vastly different from these childhood fantasies.

We're not always the heroes of the game, and we are not always the survivors of catastrophes. Surviving a catastrophe requires preparation—just as we practice and prepare to hit a home run or save the kingdom. This short book will help you prepare for—and survive— most catastrophic natural or man-made disasters along Colorado's Front Range. There are many risks in living, but we can prepare for most of these dangers without undue obsession. Floods, blizzards, chemical emergencies, fires, earthquakes, electromagnetic pulses (EMPs), pandemics, and wars are the topics of this manual.

I hope you find this work helpful. It is intended as an introduction to emergency preparation for people living along the Front Range, but it should also be helpful to those who live on the Western Slope.

Good luck!
Ronald T. Collins

CHAPTER 1

DISASTER RISK AND THE BASICS

There is a saying among emergency professionals that "it's not a matter of 'if'; it's a matter of when." This adage reflects the reason every person should prepare for the unexpected and the unlikely. Ask your friends what types of disasters they have experienced or have narrowly missed. I suspect you will hear stories of floods, fires, explosions, tornadoes, and numerous other near misses. You don't think it can happen here? Read on.

According to the Colorado Geological Survey website, there have been more than seven hundred large tremors in the state since 1867! The largest known earthquake occurred near Fort Collins in 1882 with an approximate magnitude of 6.6. The most economically destructive quake in Colorado history occurred in the Denver area in 1967. Even as I write these words, a magnitude 3.6

quake is being reported east of Salida! Imagine today's destructive consequences of another 6.6 earthquake centered in the Front Range population corridor along I-25. How long might you have to wait to receive water, food, shelter, or first aid?

Not worried about earthquakes? How about tornadoes? Weld County has experienced at least 268 tornadoes since 1950. Do you remember the Windsor tornado of 2008? In addition, floods are another persistent problem in Colorado and across the nation. In the 2013 floods, the affected area stretched from Colorado Springs to Fort Collins and caused the deaths of at least eight people and more than a billion dollars of damage! Think it cannot happen again? That is wishful thinking!

How about disasters caused by people? Do you really believe they cannot happen to you? Are you close to a railroad where hazardous materials are transported? In 2013, a freight train in Canada exploded in a small Quebec town. Forty-two people died, and the explosion destroyed half the downtown center. Most populated areas along the Front Range are close to rail lines. Of course, hazardous materials disasters are usually unintentional. However, people—and nations—sometimes cause intentional disasters. Will North Korea detonate nuclear weapons over the United States? Will terrorists explode such a weapon here? Will another enemy nation attack us or explode an EMP weapon over us? If history is our guide, then the answer is yes. And, of course, Colorado is a prime military target.

What about a pandemic? Colorado was hit hard in the 1918 flu pandemic, and today, some military strategists believe a nuclear attack might be coordinated with a biological attack. Of course, this is independent from a naturally occurring pandemic believed to be long overdue. How would you and your family survive if you were afraid to leave your home?

Disasters are a part of the human experience. We hope they will not affect us, but that hope is wishful thinking. It does not always happen to other people; sometimes we are the other person.

Basic Preparation

In the event of any catastrophic event, your survival will depend on many factors. Some of these factors are uncontrollable, but we must plan on circumstances where you and your family can improve the chances of surviving.

An important factor in surviving a catastrophic disaster is physical location. Under most circumstances, sheltering in place is the best decision. However, if you are not prepared, this action may simply delay the inevitable. Therefore, every person should anticipate multiple scenarios. We will address whether to shelter-in-place or evacuate in a later chapter. Regardless of the situation, the basic, prudent action *now* is to assemble a survival kit for your car, for your work, for your person, and for your home. Clearly, your home kit should be more extensively stocked than kits for your other locations. Your first priority should be to construct a home survival kit for you and your family to use when sheltering in place.

The home survival kit must be viewed as your most important physical survival asset. The home kit should include water, food, a first aid kit, and other supplies designed to support you for seventy-two hours to two weeks. Experts have different suggestions for the contents of such kits, but a bare minimum is one gallon of water per person per day and enough food to last for at least seventy-two hours.

Although I suggest planning for longer than seventy-two hours, preparing for longer time periods can be expensive. In my experience, most homes have enough food to last several days without any additional purchases. For this survival calculation, only include food not dependent on refrigeration. If you plan to survive for longer than a few days or weeks, you should purchase significant amounts of canned foods, food in bulk, and freeze-dried foods in bulk. To estimate the amount of food you should store, use a minimum calorie count of 1,100 calories per day for women and 1,300 calories per day for men. These calorie estimates are the average minimum counts to remain healthy. At those levels, most people will slowly lose weight. Costco, Sam's Club, online specialty stores, and most sporting goods stores sell freeze-dried food containers that will provide hundreds of acceptable meals. These freeze-dried foods will survive for at least two decades in a normal basement or closet. In my home, we have two months of food, twenty-eight gallons of water in seven-gallon camping containers, and enough protein bars to last at least three days. This is in addition to our normal household inventory.

Water storage can be a particular problem. Water weighs approximately eight pounds per gallon and can be difficult to carry or transport. Containers holding five to seven gallons each are available at sporting goods stores and some hardware stores. Additionally, you should purchase a food-grade emergency water container for your bathtub. For example, the commercially available WaterBOB system is placed in a bathtub, connected to the spout, and then filled with one hundred gallons of potable water. In a major disaster, this strange system could keep you alive for months. Other helpful devices providing water include LifeStraws and water purification tablets. LifeStraws are inexpensive (about twenty dollars) and resemble thick drinking straws. They will purify about a thousand gallons of water in an emergency. Hikers and campers frequently use them, and they are very convenient. LifeStraws should also be included in your automobile and work survival kits.

In your home survival kit, you have space to expand your survival equipment. Keep a good survival how-to book in that kit. I suggest your first book should be the *Boy Scout Handbook*! Don't laugh—this is a great source of general survival information. In addition, I suggest a Red Cross first aid manual and any of Creek Stewart's survival manuals. Your home kit should also include an LED flashlight and a selection of new batteries of different sizes. Do not forget candles, butane lighters, and matches. Also include a battery/solar-powered weather radio, and N-95 medical face masks, which can be found at any pharmacy or grocery store.

Don't forget a nonelectric can opener and a camping knife. Do not scrimp on a knife. A full-tang knife, similar to a military Ka-Bar, is an essential survival tool. The survival knife I keep in my SUV is a full-tang blade—meaning the metal shaft extends the entire length of the knife—and it includes a flint to ignite an outdoor fire. As long as you are spending money, you should purchase a multi-tool. I suggest a Leatherman. Multi-tools are handy under any circumstance and should be included in your auto and work kits. The last major asset included in your home kit must be a good first aid kit.

In many disaster scenarios, you must anticipate injuries to yourself or other people. You can easily purchase a prepackaged first aid kit, but these kits are not always properly stocked for some types of disasters. I suggest purchasing a multiday kit from Adventure Medical Kits and then customizing the kit. Kits should include some medical tools, including scissors and tweezers. In addition, do not forget dental supplies! Simple dental emergency kits are inexpensive and available online or at most sporting goods stores. I also include multivitamins in this discussion in case of a long-term nutritional need.

In case of a major injury, your kit should include duct tape, a tourniquet, QuikClot, and a SAM Splint. Duct tape is a universal solution to many problems, tourniquets can save a life in severe limb injury bleeding cases, QuikClot will help stop life-threatening torso bleeding, and a SAM Splint stabilizes broken bones. In conjunction with your first aid kit, you should be trained in first aid. Complete a basic first aid class and then take a wilderness first aid class. The basic first aid class does not really train you for an extended separation from emergency medical services, but wilderness classes train you to provide emergency first aid while anticipating a significant delay in professional medical response. First aid training is a very important element in your survival preparation.

After you have completed your home survival kit, it is time to work on your auto kit and your work kit. Your auto kit should be a smaller version of your home kit that is adapted to the special needs of your automobile. Unlike your home kit, the auto kit must also prepare for a vehicle breakdown. The auto kit should include a first aid kit, water, food, a folding shovel, kitty litter, Fix-a-Flat, a wool blanket and/or emergency space blanket, a camping knife or machete, an emergency poncho, and a backpack. Most people keep these supplies in the backpack. The backpack can be used to hike back to your home if necessary—or to a temporary, safer location. Nevertheless, remember that in most circumstances, you are usually better off remaining in your vehicle and waiting for rescue. My wife also keeps a pair of hiking shoes in her car in case of a long or cold hike to safety. Personally, I also keep emergency toilet paper in my car!

The work kit is different. Space is limited, and you do not want to be seen by coworkers as eccentric. Many people now bring small backpacks to work, and they are perfect for small emergency kits. Otherwise, I suggest preplacing your emergency supplies in your desk, locker, or other personal space. In your work kit, try to include at least six food bars, a one-quart canteen (or bottled water), rolled gauze, a Swiss Army knife, a Leatherman, cash, a tactical pen, and a small LED flashlight. Tactical pens are working pens constructed of steel and may be used as a weapon. Frequently these pens also include a small light at the top. If you work in a high-rise building, keep a pair of athletic shoes or hiking boots at work. I worked in the World Trade Center in Manhattan prior to 9/11, and you might need to exit the building and traverse debris and glass. Remember, the goal of a work kit is to get you safely out of your building.

For most people, the work kit will help you survive if you cannot leave your employment location. It will also assist in reaching your car or truck. When you can reach your car, you can consolidate the work and auto kits. If necessary, you will likely be well prepared to either hike or drive home. Emergency kits are essential, especially if surprised by an unexpected disaster. However, what if you have advance warning of a calamity with time to choose a course of action?

Stay or Go?

Survival in any catastrophe is the result of good planning, active preparation, and luck. Most catastrophic events will have at least a short warning period, but sometimes, you will just have to spontaneously react. With any immediate warning, or even a longer-term warning, the first decision you might have to consider is whether to shelter in place or evacuate.

Sheltering in place is the best possible reaction to most emergencies. An exception to this rule is when you need to escape from imminent danger. For example, staying in your house when a fire is rushing toward your home is a deadly response to a dangerous fire. On the other hand, staying in your home would likely be the best response in the case of a blizzard. It is better to be in a safe structure with food, water, and other supplies than stranded on foot or in a car.

Sheltering in place is not always an option. What happens if a disaster occurs while you are at work or in your car? All of these locations should be prepared for unexpected emergencies. Clearly, space and locale are preparation issues at settings other than your home, but there are simple precautions that can dramatically increase the likelihood of surviving a disaster.

Your home should be able to support you for a minimum of seventy-two hours. Emergency supplies in your car and at work should support you for twenty-four to seventy-two hours. Remember, the rule of thumb is to have one gallon of water per person for each day in each location. Also, have enough food to support essential calorie demand for each person in your group. Usually this is around two thousand calories per person per day in stressful circumstances. Daily consumption of 1,100–1,300 calories is more of a survival/subsistence level. An easy way to accomplish this goal for your car and business in short-term circumstances is to use high-quality protein bars.

An essential survival tool for both sheltering in place

and for evacuations is a first aid kit. Prepare to spend money with this purchase. Your life, and the lives of your family and friends, may depend on your first aid kit and your expertise with basic first aid. We are not primarily concerned with injuries requiring Band-Aids. Look for more advanced kits for wilderness first aid, and do not forget to purchase QuikClot and SAM Splints. Two excellent sources for these supplies include REI and Adventure Medical Kits. Also, do not overlook my advice to take two first aid classes, including a basic first aid class and a wilderness first aid class. Two excellent training sources for both these classes are the Red Cross and the Colorado Mountain Club.

Evacuating from a dangerous location is an alternative to sheltering in place. The authorities may even require you to evacuate, but usually you might decide evacuation is the prudent action. You may or may not have time to plan your evacuation. In every circumstance, you must plan for the worst. Assume you will not have more than a few minutes to plan your evacuation. This means you must have easily accessible supplies ready to go. "Preppers" usually refer to these kits as *bug-out bags*. They are backpacks or other containers that will support you after you leave your home. Bug-out bags should contain emergency food, water, first aid supplies, and other items that will help you survive in the coming days. Prudence dictates you should also have the equivalent of a bug-out bag in your car and at your work. If you evacuate using your vehicle, you will eventually be able to combine the resources of your home kit and the kit in your car.

Whether sheltering in place or evacuating, a key survival tool is your car. Your car is basic to surviving a disaster. It can act as shelter, a source of warmth, storage for supplies, and transportation to help you escape danger. This reliance upon your car means it must be prepared for multiple types of disasters. A basic survival principle is to always keep at least half a tank of gas in case you need to leave your shelter or your work. Keep your tires in good condition; I suggest tires appropriate for off-road driving. Buy an SUV in lieu of more standard passenger sedans. Always keep emergency supplies in your car. Your car emergency kit should include a seventy-two-hour supply of emergency food and at least one gallon of water. Don't forget a normal winter emergency kit. For suggested supplies, see the appendix at the conclusion of this book.

The last basic rule concerns your physical condition. Emergencies always place additional stress on our bodies. Your survival may hinge on your ability to survive difficult physical challenges. If you do not exercise, you are probably aerobically unfit. In addition, if you are overweight, you may experience difficulties you are unable to overcome. A person does not have to be a jock, a weightlifter, or a skinny marathon runner to improve his or her chances of survival in an emergency. The important issue is aerobic conditioning. If you do not exercise now, start walking regularly or use a treadmill or an elliptical. The same holds true for overweight individuals. Overweight does not necessarily mean out of shape. Make yourself aerobically fit regardless of your weight because your survival might depend on your fitness.

Your body, your car, your bug-out bag, and your home must be prepared to survive a disaster. Now let us get into some specifics.

Evacuation

Moving out of the way of danger is an essential strategy in your disaster response. Natural disasters and man-made catastrophes may require you to either immediately relocate or relocate after the initial event. Even if you survive the immediate threat, your long-term survival may still be in doubt.

We should look at short-term evacuations as situations where there is an immediate threat to your safety, but there is not long-term danger. For example, floods, chemicals, and tornadoes are short-term threats. However, certain types of chemicals may present long-term hazards beyond the immediate danger. If possible, the best response is to leave your current location immediately and move to a safe point. In the case of this type of threat, have a bug-out kit available and hit the road or get to cover! You want to have a bag in case your shelter is destroyed or if you need first aid supplies. Specific advice on bug-out kits is included in a later chapter.

Long-term evacuation is a more complicated, serious, and dangerous action. In our discussion, LTE should be reserved for war, civil unrest, or catastrophic disaster. There are three primary components in LTE. These include transportation, supplies, and a destination.

For both short- and long-term evacuations, you must have transportation. In most cases, this will be your automobile. In the case of an EMP event, your vehicle has about a 15–20 percent chance of becoming completely disabled according to some studies. This probability increases if the vehicle is operating at the moment of an EMP. An EMP is a side effect of a nuclear reaction and caused by the sun or by nuclear weapons. An EMP caused by the sun is likely to provide some warning, perhaps days in advance, but an EMP caused by a nuclear weapon might only be preceded by a warning of a few minutes prior to the weapon's detonation. The important point is to remember to keep your transportation fueled, in good repair, and stocked with your survival kit.

Regardless of the circumstances, you cannot evacuate if you do not have fuel. Always keep at least half a tank of gas in your car. Always keep your car in good repair. Make certain the battery is reliable. Place mud and snow tires on the vehicle. You can purchase mud and snow tires that look similar to normal tires if that concerns you. Get rid of the miniature spare tire—and replace it with a full-size spare. In the event of a catastrophic disaster, a flimsy temporary spare may not last long enough to help save you. Keep a fire extinguisher in your vehicle along with a first aid kit. Also, I suggest you subscribe to satellite radio. The local AM/FM stations may be off the air, and if your radio will still function, your only source of information might be from satellite radio. Keep in mind that along the Front Range, KOA AM at 850 is an official emergency broadcast station. In addition, keep basic repair tools in your car, including a jack and Fix-a-Flat.

Related to keeping a fire extinguisher and can of Fix-a-Flat in your car is the need to keep other essential supplies there too. You should always keep a bug-out bag in your house with a similar kit in each car. If nothing else, purchase a seventy-two-hour emergency backpack from the American Red Cross website. Add additional supplies to the Red Cross backpack from the suggestions listed later in the book. It is especially important to add a supply of water to your supplies. Most people need to drink around a half gallon of fluids daily, but the recommended minimum is one gallon. Therefore, two two-quart canteens of water per person should be viewed as a minimum requirement to keep in your car.

In addition to repair tools and water, there are other essential items to keep in your car: jumper cables, flares, energy bars, a flashlight, duct tape, wool and space blankets, a first aid kit, and warm clothing. A multi-tool is a good but expensive investment for your car. Also, some type of protection might come in handy. For example, a Ka-Bar fixed-blade knife would be a good addition to your supplies.

Where do you keep this small collection of supplies? Purchase a plastic container to hold your supplies in your trunk. Manufacturers produce specific products for this purpose. I have seen this type of container at Walmart, Lowe's, and Home Depot. To help prevent theft of your supplies, use the wool blanket to cover your supplies if they are visible.

The final consideration in your evacuation plan is your destination. Where will you go? In the event of a catastrophic event, there might be a mass exodus along the Front Range—all heading for the mountains. Do you want to be there with thousands of unprepared, desperate people? A safe strategy might be to only associate with friends and avoid all strangers. An argument can be made that going east onto the plains could be a safer strategy in certain situations. Your decision in this matter depends on the crisis. If there seems to be an impending enemy attack, you want to avoid likely targets. That means you cannot go east toward our missile silos, you cannot head south toward Colorado Springs, and you cannot head north toward Cheyenne and Warren Air Force Base! If you head west, it might be you and your closest million friends. Also, keep paper maps in your vehicle. GPS systems might be unavailable.

Whatever your destination, plan carefully. Try to preselect a location near water. Do not wait until the last minute if possible. Avoid the crowds. People expect things to remain the same, which is called *normalcy bias*, and they will wait until the last minute to evacuate or buy supplies, thereby creating chaos, gridlock, and shortages! Work on developing a network of friends with similar views who can rendezvous at an agreed-upon location. If you do not know anyone of similar mind, investigate MeetUp.com to find a group of like-minded people. Then, take your bug-out kit from your home to add to the one in your car. Be quick, be careful, and be prepared.

Transportation

Mobility in a catastrophic disaster might save your life. Either going home or leaving home to find a safer location might be necessary. Either of these actions requires dependable transportation.

In the best situation, anyone interested in surviving a catastrophic disaster would drive a four-wheel drive, off-road, fully stocked vehicle. Nevertheless, reality has a way of intruding on these desires. If you have such a vehicle, you are ahead of the game. If, like most people, you are lacking such a vehicle, there are a few steps you can take to improve your situation. First, always carry your auto emergency kit in the vehicle. Second, switch your tires to off-road mud and snow tires. Third, add skid plates to the underside of your vehicle. Fourth, purchase a cargo carrier for your vehicle, and fifth, keep at least half a tank in your vehicle at all times. A cargo carrier will allow you to carry additional supplies if you evacuate, including water, food, and gasoline. Having at least a half tank of fuel means you can leave a dangerous situation if necessary and will not be waiting in a line for rationed— or nonexistent—fuel. Do not depend on purchasing gas en route. There are about seven thousand gas stations in Colorado, and approximately seven of them have backup generators! Without electricity they cannot pump fuel.

A few other improvements to your vehicle might also come in handy in a catastrophe. A trailer hitch could be immensely helpful if you evacuate. A brush guard will protect your radiator and front end. A full-size spare tire could save your life if you only have one of the mini-sized spares. A CB radio or a HAM transceiver could give you communication access. Of the two, a HAM mobile transceiver is the better choice. A handheld transceiver would also work, and it would be more mobile if you leave your vehicle. Keep your vehicle properly maintained—and do not draw attention to the vehicle by openly displaying your supplies. I added a false bottom in my SUV's storage area and covered it with a dark blanket. The supplies are not invisible, but they are difficult to see. If you evacuate, your vehicle might be the tool that either ensures your survival or ensures your demise. Balance the scales in favor of survival.

Other means of transportation include motorcycles, scooters, and bicycles. Bicycles offer reliable transport, especially if the disaster is an EMP and your vehicle is inoperable. If you elect to use a bicycle as a backup, or even as a primary means of mobility, do not depend on a road bike. A decent mountain bike will carry you and your supplies. Additionally, you will not be restricted to traveling on paved surfaces. Some disasters may damage roads and streets, but mountain bikes can follow alternate paths. Another factor to consider is traffic congestion. In the event of a catastrophe with warning, many people will evacuate along the Front Range. This means I-25, I-70, and I-76 might be mobbed with vehicles. Your worst nightmare is being caught in the open—in stalled traffic—with millions of scared strangers.

Be realistic, but always consider a worst-case scenario when facing a disaster. Sheltering in place is usually the best choice, and it keeps you away from crowds and off the interstate highways. If you have to bug out (evacuate), try to use little-known roads and act before everyone else. Finally, keep your vehicle gassed (or charged) up. Never let your fuel fall below half a tank. Be ready!

CHAPTER 2

NATURAL DISASTERS

<u>Floods</u>

Since you live in Colorado, you know the danger of a flood. The floods of 2013 shocked us all, and there were some valuable lessons we had to learn. Lesson number one: Do not underestimate the force of moving water. Lesson number two: Buy flood insurance. Lesson number three: Be prepared to evacuate.

Floods have the distinction of being the most frequent and financially costly natural disasters in the United States. According to the United States Geological Survey, floods account for more than 75 percent of declared federal disasters. Basic rules in dealing with floods include not buying or building in a floodplain, but this does not guarantee you will be able to avoid being flooded. Also, be aware of the differences between a flood watch and a flood warning. A warning means a flood is occurring or will soon occur. A watch means conditions are favorable for flooding.

What should you do if you are outside—or in your car—when a warning is broadcast or you see evidence of a flood? Quickly get to high ground. If you have a few minutes to prepare your home, cut the electricity to your house at the main circuit breaker and then evacuate. Be aware of flood risk if you are experiencing heavy rain in a short time, if there is news of a dam break, and during the spring snowmelt. Do not enter your basement to throw your electrical breaker if the basement is flooded.

If you are caught outside during a flood, try to avoid walking through moving water. Depending on your size and strength, as little as four to six inches of water can cause you to fall. Remember that important fact if you have children with you. With a child's smaller mass and weaker body strength, relatively shallow flooding can cause children to fall into floodwaters. Another reason to improve your physical fitness is because you may have to carry your children or grandchildren.

The rapid flow of floodwater also carries dangerous debris, and two feet of fast-moving water can carry away most vehicles. In addition, if you are exposed to floodwater, you must make certain your tetanus shots are current. Tetanus is a vicious, deadly bacterial infection. The infection is frequently associated with rusty nails, but rust is not the cause of the infection. The tetanus bacteria are common around the world, and vaccinations are the only protection. If you are exposed to floodwater, you have probably been exposed to tetanus. Contact your medical provider as soon as possible. Also, do not drink any unpurified flood water; it will be contaminated with both natural and artificial toxins. Bottled water is your best choice during this type of emergency.

After a flood, your priority is your health and the health of your family. See your medical provider immediately. Use common sense. Avoid downed power lines and any remaining floodwater—stagnant or moving. Remember, there may be other pollutants in the water besides natural contaminants. Be cautious of areas affected by the flooding. The water may have weakened roads, boulders, and bridges. Sewage systems will probably be compromised, which expands the range of possible health problems. If there is any possibility the city water supply is contaminated, boil all water and use filters similar to a LifeStraw. Do not return to your home until the local authorities have given you permission.

Floods are the most common natural disasters in the United States. Do not underestimate their destructive power or lingering effects. Moreover, as you repair your home, remember that those dangerous contaminants are still in the water, debris, and mud you are removing. The best preparation for flooding is to avoid being in a floodplain and evacuating as soon as possible.

Fires

Colorado is unique in many ways when the discussion concerns fires. Coloradans must be concerned with house fires and forest fires. Like floods, fires are hard to predict, are excruciatingly dangerous, and are difficult to prepare for. In reality, the best preparation for fires is to prevent them.

The basic rules for fire survival are to keep your home properly maintained, remove unnecessary fuel sources (papers, rags, etc.), shut off utilities when appropriate, and strategically place fire extinguishers throughout your residence. Fire requires heat, fuel, and oxygen to combust, and heat and fuel are easier to control than the oxygen supply in most circumstances. Fire consumes oxygen, which explains why asphyxiation is the most common cause of death from fire.

In case of a fire, you want to quickly exit any burning structure. Do not forget to make a family escape plan. Keep fire ladders for upper rooms in your home or business. You must keep flammable materials away from electrical outlets and other sources of heat. Make certain your wiring and outlets work properly and place smoke and carbon monoxide alarms throughout the house. If you have an older home, have an electrician inspect your house to determine if upgrades are necessary for your safety.

Every residence has fire hazards. The most common hazards include electrical hazards, natural gas hazards, and flammable or combustible liquids hazards. Basic fire prevention includes not smoking inside your home, keeping space heaters at least three feet from potential fuel (drapes, trash, cloth, etc.), wearing short sleeves or tight clothing when cooking, and keeping fire extinguishers within easy reach. In the event of a home fire, a proper extinguisher can help you stop a small fire before it becomes a large disaster.

Purchase the best equipment when it comes to home fire extinguishers. At the very least, you need a fully charged extinguisher in your kitchen, your garage, your upper floors, and your bedroom. Make sure your device is approved for common types of home fires; most home fire extinguishers are rated ABC, which means they will not extinguish combustible metals or cooking oils. A careful person will also practice with an extinguisher since home fire extinguishers are usually dry chemical devices and not water devices. If you have to use an extinguisher, *point* toward the base of the fire, *pull* the pin, *squeeze* the trigger, and *sweep* the fire (PASS). If the fire is not extinguished after five seconds, leave the scene—and close the doors behind you! By practicing, you will quickly learn how effective extinguishers can be, you and will also learn their drawbacks.

Besides fire extinguishers, every home should have smoke and carbon monoxide detectors. The best plan is to have these devices installed by an alarm company that can alert your local fire department if activated. Other helpful tools for fires are whistles and hammers in every room. Any family member should use a whistle as soon as that person detects a house fire. This might awaken any other family members in the house and provide them time to escape. In addition, keep interior doors closed at night. Closed doors will help keep heat, smoke, and deadly gases out of bedrooms, which can give you a little extra time to escape. In a fire, time is essential. Do not waffle. Get out! Do not get dressed, do not search for your pet, and do not get your valuables. Just get out! Keep a hammer in your room in case you need to knock out a window to escape. If you sleep upstairs, keep a fire emergency ladder to drop out of your window to climb down. Fires are fast and unpredictable. You cannot waste time.

In the case of an electrical fire, shut off the power at the central breaker; for a natural gas leak or fire, shut off the gas at the gas meter. Electrical fires present the additional risk of electrocution, and you should not enter a flooded basement to cut power or walk through other areas with standing water. Water conducts electricity and must be avoided in the case of an electrical problem.

Natural gas hazards are significant due to the explosive potential of the gas and its ability to asphyxiate. Additionally, natural gas presents a wider risk as it endangers nearby structures because of its extreme explosive capability. Furnaces, hot water heaters, dryers, stoves, and gas appliances can be natural gas hazards. Locate your shut-off valve for gas and keep a pair of spark-resistant pliers nearby in case you need to close the valve. If you have a shut-off valve in your basement, I recommend having a professional relocate the device outside and above ground. Your local power company will arrange this important change. Lastly, if you shut off the gas, you must have the gas company restart it.

Forest fires are a completely different issue. Forest fire prevention is frequently beyond the control of a homeowner. Fire mitigation is a separate issue, and homeowners should use fire mitigation strategies suggested by the Fire Service. Rangers and local fire services will happily visit your structure to advise you on fire prevention and mitigation.

Never underestimate the speed and ferocity of wildfires. According to some experts, wildfires can progress between seven and fourteen miles per hour, making it impossible to outrun most fires. They are also notoriously unpredictable in terms of direction. When warned of a possible forest fire, secure your home and then leave. In the meantime, construct any new home using fire-resistant materials and allow for defensible spaces around any structure.

The important point for fires is to prevent them and be prepared to evacuate.

Pandemic

Probably one of the most difficult disasters to prepare for is also one of the scariest. A pandemic is the spread of any infectious disease across a very large geographical region. The difference between pandemics and epidemics is the size of the affected area. Unfortunately, these events are recurring experiences in history, and we are long overdue for a catastrophic outbreak.

The rapid and extensive spread of disease can be either a natural event or the result of a biological attack. Either way, your interest is served by being properly prepared. The infamous influenza pandemic of 1918 came in multiple waves across the globe and eventually killed almost one hundred million people! Although the 1918 flu is frequently called the Spanish flu, current scientific opinion is that it actually originated in Kansas and then spread around the globe. By some estimates, the Black Death of the Middle Ages killed half the population of Europe. These two pandemics are the most infamous in world history, but by no means are they the only such events. For our purposes, we are more concerned with the circumstances of the 1918 flu pandemic, which is more likely to resemble today's danger than the Black Death.

Interestingly, one of the more successful reports of minimizing the spread of the 1918 flu pandemic comes from Colorado. As the influenza spread across the country in the first wave, the little mountain town of Gunnison was almost unaffected. How did this happen? It turns out that Gunnison decided to quarantine itself. They refused to allow people into the town and thereby eliminated the primary cause of contagion: infected travelers and miners.

The lesson from Gunnison is simple. In the event of a disastrous outbreak of disease, isolate yourself. This means staying in your home and only leaving if your life depends on leaving that safe spot. This is another reason to have adequate food and water in your home shelter. If you are forced to leave the house, take safety measures. Wear your N-95 face mask, wear gloves, do not touch your face with your hands, do not shake hands with people, and thoroughly wash your hands upon your return.

To protect yourself inside your home, take the same precautions you would in the event of a threatening chemical leak or nuclear fallout. Turn off heating and air-conditioning, close fireplace dampers, and lock all exterior doors and windows. Then cover all exterior windows and doors with plastic sheets from inside your location. Seal around the plastic with duct tape. In addition, do not forget any heating or air-conditioning vents in the rooms. Close the vents and then seal them with the plastic sheets and duct tape.

If it is winter or summer, you must prepare for those conditions. Since the electricity will probably be working, have an emergency electric heater or a propane camping heater. Also, have electric fans you can use for high heat in the summer. Advertisers promote propane heaters as safe for indoor use, but I would still invest in a carbon-monoxide alarm just in case. Always assume indoor flames are dangerous sources of fire and poisonous gases. Portable electric heaters are the preferred choice if you do not have a fireplace and still have electricity.

A pandemic is most likely to be an event caused by nature. However, some military strategists have suggested a nuclear attack could be coordinated with a biological attack. The theory is that survivors of a nuclear attack will be subject to a biological attack as they start to emerge from shelters. Many people will have weakened immune systems from lack of food and exposure to radiation, which makes them more susceptible to infection by a biological weapon. A dangerous disease could then infect their weakened immune systems.

What is our conclusion regarding preparing for a pandemic? Have water, food, plastic sheets (heavy-duty garbage bags), duct tape, multivitamins, a complete first aid kit, N-95 masks, and antibiotics. Additionally, have backup systems to warm and cool your home.

CHAPTER 3

MAN-MADE DISASTERS

<u>Hazardous Materials</u>

Human-caused disasters are a constant feature in our lives. As industrial societies become more complex, they are also more prone to periodic failures of parts of their structure. For example, as population increases, there is greater demand for chemicals in manufacturing. These chemicals are transported via trucks and trains. Occasionally these transports crash or have other problems that cause chemical spills or explosions and endanger our lives. This is an unpleasant fact, but it is not limited to chemical spills.

Chemical spills are an important risk, but other man-made risks include nuclear explosions, civil disorder, war, and biological hazards. Keep in mind that chemical spills, nuclear accidents, and biological hazards usually do not allow predictable preparatory time. The nature of accidents limits warning time. On the other hand, war, nuclear attacks, civil disorder, and biological attacks might allow people to prepare in advance. Terrorist actions, however, might not give you adequate notice. In the case of war or a nuclear attack, there would probably be weeks of increased global tension, which would allow you time to improve your preparation. *Fortunately, preparation for one disaster also works to prepare you for most other disasters.*

Chemical spills and chemical attacks are some of the most difficult hazards to face. You might not be able to see or even smell a life-threatening chemical. Complicating the problem is that these dangerous products are frequently transported in railcars or trucks near population centers. Consequently, you may have only seconds to protect yourself and your family.

Chemical hazards are difficult to detect and deflect. One of the best techniques for protecting yourself is to have a *safe room* in your residence. A safe room is a confined space that offers protection and the ability to seal any entrance. Since chemicals usually drift down toward the earth, higher elevations are safer than lower elevations. Therefore, for chemical hazards, do not go to your basement! Instead, try to use the highest point in your home that you can seal against the outside.

In your chemical safe room (probably a closet), keep a supply of duct tape and sheets of plastic or plastic trash bags. Use the tape and plastic to cover the doors and any other possible entrance for outside gases. If you live near railroad tracks or an interstate highway, I suggest NBC masks for each family member. NBC stands for nuclear, biological, and chemical. The Israelis are experts in this type of equipment, and there are many online sources for these masks. Do not buy older models or used ones. Once you are in your safe room and have sealed the doors and windows, do not sit! As strange as it sounds, you should elevate yourself as high as possible since dangerous gases have a tendency to settle near ground level. Bring chairs, ladders, or stools into the safe room and stand on them.

Chemical accidents are more common than most people realize. Additionally, they can be catastrophic events, which the people of Bhopal, India, discovered in 1984. The Bhopal disaster is a good example of the dangers of location, among other issues. More than half a million people were injured—and thousands were killed—in this chemical tragedy.

Chemical disasters are not restricted to developing nations. In 2013, Canada experienced an oil train derailment and explosion that killed forty-seven people and destroyed a significant portion of a town. Do you live near a railroad, an airport, or an industrial park? Do not think it can never happen in your neighborhood.

The other major type of man-made disaster we will address is the issue of nuclear materials. I think this issue is so significant that I have included it in the chapter concerning nuclear war.

War
___

Some experts separate disasters into low-impact/high-probability or high-impact/low-probability events. High-impact/low-probability events include cosmic collisions, a Yellowstone eruption, a solar EMP, or nuclear war. However, for various reasons, some experts consider the possibility of nuclear war to be higher now than in past decades. Planning to survive a catastrophic disaster requires you to plan for a nuclear explosion and its aftermath. The advantage of preparing for nuclear war is these preparations will also prepare you for almost all other catastrophic events.

Many Americans consider the possibility of a nuclear war to be low or virtually impossible. They think it is irrational and that people across the world are all rational—like we consider ourselves rational. This is nonsense! War is seldom rational, and history is rife with proof: World War I, World War II, Korea, Vietnam, Iraq, 9/11, and Afghanistan.

Regardless of whether any particular war is rational, the sad reality is that wars happen. Today, some military leaders consider the likelihood of war increasing to its highest probability in decades. The Bulletin of Atomic Scientists agrees and recently moved the Doomsday Clock closer to midnight than it has been since 1953! The reasons for this change center around improved technology and other factors.

Weapons targeting systems and global positioning systems (GPS) are much more accurate than in the past.

This increased accuracy means nuclear weapons can have a successful mission with reduced explosive force and reduced long-term environmental damage. These smaller, more accurate weapons can accomplish missions that previously required larger and more numerous nuclear weapons. Additionally, Russia has changed its previous policy of "no first use" of nuclear weapons. Russia now considers use of smaller, tactical nuclear weapons to be part of their normal battle plans. They feel escalation to strategic nuclear weapons is unlikely. Western nations think any use of nuclear weapons would quickly escalate to strategic weapons and global nuclear war. Wow.

Another common American attitude is a fatalistic one: "I don't want to survive an attack, so I will do nothing and just die." One of the many problems with this attitude is that you might not have a choice about surviving an initial attack. Most Americans would survive a nuclear attack. If you had not prepared for an emergency, you might die later of painful injuries, starvation, dehydration, or radiation poisoning. Preparing for a nuclear attack requires only minor additions to your normal disaster preparation—and you do not want to be sitting in your house after an attack watching your family die because you were stupid.

Our first preparation step is to look at likely targets of a nuclear attack. Colorado Springs, Denver, and Cheyenne are clear priority targets. Denver's primary attraction as a potential target comes from being a population center. Colorado Springs, Denver International Airport, Buckley Air Force Base, and Cheyenne, Wyoming, are also military targets. Your proximity to these targets will determine the course of your planning.

Most current nuclear weapons contain around three hundred to six hundred kilotons of explosive force. The Hiroshima and Nagasaki detonations were ten to twenty-two kilotons each. A kiloton is equivalent to one thousand tons of TNT, and a megaton is equivalent to one million tons of TNT. Still, today's nukes are considerably smaller than previous generations of weapons, due to improved targeting abilities, and they no longer necessarily rely on explosive force measured in megatons.

To help in preparing for a possible nuclear attack, visit NUKEMAP on the internet. You will be able to determine the likely damage in your area from any attack. This website allows you to control the size of the weapon to help determine the relative safety of your location in different scenarios. Remember, unlike what the urban myths say, surviving a nuclear explosion is both possible and likely. If you survive the initial attack and are properly prepared to survive the next few weeks, your biggest concern will be surviving the resulting long-term aftermath.

If a nuclear detonation occurs, it is likely you will have advance notice. International tensions will probably have risen, and there will be talk of war. There might even be a specific incident that is causing the tensions. Don't waste time! Humans have a tendency to believe things will continue as they have been. We deny the possibility of rapid, disruptive change. Think independently and act. At the moment of nuclear detonation, you will no longer be able to prepare. Procrastination might kill you.

At the moment of detonation, duck and cover. Contrary to comedian jokes, this technique actually works. A small number of Japanese survivors of the Hiroshima attack were unfortunate enough to also be in Nagasaki for that attack. They survived the Nagasaki attack by utilizing duck and cover. This helped them avoid thermal radiation (heat) and helped avoid projectiles (primarily glass); both effects were major causes of fatalities in the bombings. Robert Trumbull relays details of the survivors of Hiroshima, who were also caught in Nagasaki, in his book *Nine Who Survived Hiroshima and Nagasaki.*

Your goal in preparing to survive a nuclear detonation is to protect yourself from heat, blast, and radiation. Nuclear weapons can detonate near the earth (a surface blast), aboveground as an airburst, or as a high-altitude burst. Surface detonations are less destructive, but they may produce significant amounts of radioactive fallout. Surface explosions take material from the affected area and suck it into the upper atmosphere, and it is eventually carried by the jet stream. The material then scatters across large areas, generally to the east of the detonation site. Your immediate concern when detecting an explosion is preventing flash blindness, protecting against thermal (heat) burns, and protecting against the blast. Dealing with fallout comes later.

Airbursts are the most destructive form of explosions, but they produce reduced levels of radioactive fallout. For any type of burst, you must immediately protect your eyes against flash blindness. The luminosity of a nuclear explosion is many times that of the sun. Fortunately, it does not last very long, usually between twenty seconds and two minutes. If you anticipate a nuclear attack, try to avoid glancing in the direction of likely targets. If you are outside, always wear sunglasses—every little bit helps—and try to keep buildings or natural structures between you and the likely target. If you become aware of a flash, immediately duck and cover! If you become aware of a detonation, look away! The flash can last for enough time for you to look toward it. Don't!

Immediately upon recognizing a blast, duck behind cover or fall flat on the ground with your arms covering your head. Depending on your distance from the epicenter of the detonation and the explosive force of the weapon, you may be endangered by both heat and blast. A twenty-megaton air burst could cause severe burns twenty to twenty-five miles away; fortunately, weapons of this size have become uncommon if not obsolete.

At Hiroshima and Nagasaki, heat and flying debris were the two principal causes of death and injury. Oddly, the thermal radiation was relatively brief and easily protected against. Light-colored clothing and minimal physical barriers between the individual and the detonation prevented severe burns in most cases.

Besides protecting one's self from thermal radiation (heat), the blast is a matter of concern. If you are too close to the epicenter, you may not be able to protect yourself from the blast. However, that circumstance is unlikely. The primary concern from the blast is flying debris and structural collapse. If your house, office, or garage is capable of surviving the blast, it is likely your windows will not. In the blast danger zone, flying glass is a potent danger—if your building survives. Protect yourself by immediately ducking and finding cover. To prepare today, add protection to your windows such as plantation or hurricane shutters, and install security film on every window. Professionally installed security film will protect you from burglars and mitigate the effects of explosions. These simple actions might save your life.

Radiation is the third major risk presented by a nuclear detonation. A nuclear explosion produces alpha, beta, and gamma radiation. Thick clothing and gloves easily mitigate alpha and beta radiation effects. However, you do not want to ingest or inhale particles emitting alpha or beta radiation. Keep N-95 face masks easily accessible and avoid eating or drinking products that might be contaminated. I have found these medical masks at every pharmacy and most grocery stores. They are inexpensive, and each one only costs a few dollars. If you prefer a slight upgrade for a mask, purchase an N-100 mask. The N-100 masks are usually in the range of ten to thirteen dollars each. Protection from gamma radiation is another story in our survival plans.

Protecting against dangerous, life-threatening gamma radiation is a function of exposure time, distance, and shielding. The one variable of these three factors that we can most easily control is shielding. By controlling the amount and type of shielding, we can essentially minimize exposure time and create artificial distance. To protect against gamma radiation, thick, dense material is essential. The rule of thumb is three feet of compacted soil is required to reduce gamma exposure to survivable levels, but two feet of concrete accomplishes a similar result. Obviously, we are discussing fallout shelters when addressing issues with this type of radiation.

In the best of all possible worlds, we would all have underground, outdoor, fully stocked blast- and radiation-proof fallout shelters. However, we live in reality and not in a fantasy world. In lieu of fantasy, let us plan for reality. If you have an underground basement, you are ahead of the game. You can easily build an effective fallout shelter and stock your shelter with water, food, creature comforts, and a good first aid kit. Do not forget a portable chemical toilet, which can be found online, in outdoors stores, or at Target or Walmart. I recommend keeping all your camping equipment in the shelter.

The greatest risk with a basement shelter is if your home suffers significant structural damage or catches fire. To help prevent this possibility, immediately cut electrical power to your home at the central breaker after an attack, turn off the gas coming into your home, and turn off the city water coming into your house. Try to complete these actions prior to the event—do them upon warning. Common sense dictates keeping a fire extinguisher in your shelter and keeping other extinguishers strategically located in your house and garage. After the initial explosion, you will likely have twenty to thirty minutes to complete these important tasks.

Assuming your residence is undamaged and you do not have a basement suitable for a shelter, you can still use your home. The rule is to place the greatest mass possible between you and the source of radiation. You will need to find the innermost secure location and then place books, furniture, bricks, sandbags, and any other heavy objects on each side of your protected space. Do not forget above you too! The more material, the better. Storage space under a staircase and first-floor interior bathrooms are good. You must stay in this space for a minimum of three days (seventy-two hours). If possible, plan to stay in your shelter for two weeks. Radiation effects decay at different rates, but two weeks after the detonation, radiation levels will be approximately 1/1000 of initial levels.

Do not underestimate the difficulties of being in a shelter for three days or two weeks. What will you do about light? How will you use the bathroom? How will you handle human waste? You must plan for these issues. At least keep a five-gallon plastic bucket with enough trash bags to last for two weeks. For a basement shelter, you could have the luxury of a portable chemical toilet. The price on such products range from about fourteen dollars to almost one hundred dollars. Whether you are using a simple bucket or a more suitable chemical toilet, you must prepare yourself for the discomfort of being in such close proximity to human waste. Keep your chemical toilet simple; you do not want an expensive device to break down during the emergency. Buy double-thickness trash bags suitable for your size toilet, buy kitty litter to use for odor control, and have enough toilet paper to last your family for two weeks. If you plan to use a bucket, you should also store strong plastic trash bags with a method for sealing the bags—and do not forget the kitty litter and toilet paper. If you decide to use a simple bucket, I suggest buying a toilet seat cover, which can be found at most sporting goods stores. After three days in the shelter, you can remove the bags in a brief foray out of the shelter.

In disaster preparation, you are being prudent by anticipating the increasing likelihood of nuclear war. Analyze the risks associated with the location of your residence and your worksite by using NUKEMAP, locate the best spot in your house for a shelter, and take mitigation actions to reduce the likelihood of damage to your home by adding protection to windows and glass doors. In addition, take a wilderness first aid class, read additional material concerning nuclear weapons, and stock your shelter. In my opinion, you should stock your shelter with these materials and in this priority:

1. Water (one gallon per person per day for two weeks)
2. First aid kit (one for remote wilderness)
3. Toilet and supplies
4. Food
5. Potassium iodine tablet regimen for each family member

Remember, do not wait! In case of escalating global tensions, there might be a panic run on building materials, food, gasoline, and other essential supplies. Acting late might be acting *too* late!

Hawaii

In January 2018, we had a false warning of a ballistic missile attack on the Hawaiian Islands. Unfortunate as this experience was, it still gives us a unique opportunity to analyze a real public response to a nuclear attack and how most people will respond to any sort of imminent catastrophic disaster. Public reports of the range of responses to this false alarm included emotional, heartrending stories of phone calls to loved ones, panicked attempts to retrieve children, life-threatening driving, and even an occasional appropriate response. Happily, the alarm was incorrect, and I can find no reports of injuries or deaths as a result of the false warning.

What did people do? Some Hawaiians huddled in bathtubs just as do people in tornado-prone areas. A bathroom has extensive piping; therefore, it tends to be structurally stronger than most other areas of a residence. This is why bathrooms occasionally survive tornadoes when the rest of the structure is destroyed. Other people ran into commercial buildings or basements at work sites. This is a good idea since basements offer some protection against blast and radiation.

Witnesses also reported seeing college students running out of buildings into open areas or running between buildings. Being upright in an open area is one of the worst situations to be in when under attack or in almost any disaster. In a nuclear attack, concrete, brick, and stone buildings offer significant protection.

What about people in their vehicles? Drivers caught in

their cars and trucks were noticed speeding, abandoning vehicles, and parking inside tunnels. If caught in your car during an imminent attack, the best response is to exit the vehicle and run into a building with a solid exterior. Otherwise, exit, find a culvert or depression in the ground, and cover your head.

Other responses during the alarm included diving under tables in cafés and restaurants. If you find yourself in this situation, try to position yourself away from windows and the likely path of glass shrapnel. If possible, arrange the tables to protect against falling debris and shrapnel coming from the sides.

If you are in a residence, business, or office building and have a twenty- or thirty-minute warning, what should you do? First, turn off the utilities in the following order: gas, electricity, and water. Second, close your curtains, drapes, blinds, or shutters to diminish shrapnel. Third, go to your home shelter you have already prepared! You should have time to complete these quick actions since Colorado would normally expect a twenty- or thirty-minute notice of an external attack.

A terrorist detonating a nuclear bomb presents a more difficult situation. This scenario might provide no warning, but it would probably be a small explosion. The biggest risk for most people in that situation would be the spread of radioactive fallout. In that case, button up your location, move to your prepared shelter if possible, and listen to your radio for instructions. The Hawaii false alarm demonstrated what will happen to people with notification of an imminent catastrophic disaster. At that moment, it is too late to prepare. Instead, you must respond. Have emergency kits at home, at your job, and in your vehicle. Know the risks, be prepared, stay informed, and try not to panic if it happens to you.

EMPs

EMPs are a side effect of nuclear explosions. EMPs can occur in nature or by human design from the detonation of a nuclear weapon and are technically known as electromagnetic pulses. Either source is a formidable cause of destruction and danger.

In nature, the sun presents the greatest risk of a catastrophic, civilization-ending EMP. We are fortunate to have missed recent solar events that would have severely disrupted global dependence on electronics and electricity. An EMP is essentially an extraordinarily powerful signal that damages electronic equipment and causes electrical overloads. Power lines would act as large antennas that focus the energy.

In case of an exceptionally large solar EMP, we could expect fires caused by dangerous electrical overloads and wholesale destruction of sensitive electronics. This destruction might include communications equipment, supervisory control and data acquisition (SCADA) systems, motor vehicle ignition systems, large power transformers (LPTs), and sensitive hospital equipment. Anything electrical might be endangered.

This issue is more serious than it seems on the

surface. An EMP of this type could affect any area of the globe—or the entire globe. LPTs control the power grid, and if damaged, it takes one to two years for a foreign manufacturer to replace each unit. Some utilities have prepared for this possibility, but there are thousands of LPTs in the United States. The destruction of even a small number of these transformers would be a major disaster. If power to large areas was disrupted due to a solar EMP, imagine life without electricity. Gas could not be pumped at the gas station, homes could not be heated, lights would be useless, and refrigerators would fail—and that is the best-case scenario. Recent events in California displayed this scenario when utilities scheduled rolling blackouts.

SCADA control systems would be inoperable after an EMP. SCADA systems are essential to public health and safety, and failure of these systems would affect public water and sewer systems. SCADA systems are common electronic industrial control systems, and they are considered very vulnerable to EMPs, cyberwarfare, and cyberterrorism.

Most city water systems keep about thirty minutes of the life-essential liquid in the public water system. This is why you must keep an emergency supply of potable water. City water supplies would be unavailable if electric pumping systems are unable to operate due to power grid failure or an EMP. Additionally, if commercial transportation is unavailable, your personal supply of water might be your only reliable source. A lack of commercial transportation also means limited food supplies since grocery stores only stock about one to three days of inventory under normal circumstances. However, we have all seen what happens to grocery store inventories when people anticipate hard times. If there is advance notice of an EMP or a nuclear war, you can expect grocery shelves to be empty within hours.

EMPs caused by nuclear weapons have the same characteristic as solar EMPs. Solar-caused EMPs do not have blast, heat, and radiation effects, but they may cause extensive damage to the electrical grid. The only caveat to this is the development of nuclear weapons specifically designed to produce an enhanced EMP. These weapons detonate at high altitude, are generally of reduced explosive force, and could damage electrical/electronic equipment from Mexico City to Canada. Recent issues with North Korea have raised concerns about this topic, and that nation continues to threaten the United States with nuclear destruction.

An idiot reporter on a national cable news network claimed there was no significant risk from North Korea yet because a North Korean ICBM could not successfully reenter the atmosphere. This reporter demonstrated ignorance of the fact that a single nuclear explosion outside the atmosphere, centrally located above the center of the country, would create an EMP that would likely cause the collapse of the entire North American electrical grid and damage or destroy our electronic infrastructure.

Another concern with an EMP is the electrical overload that might result. An enhanced EMP nuclear weapon or a large solar event could produce electrical overloads on aboveground transmission lines of as much as two hundred kilovolts per meter of line. Even if this figure overestimates the overload, a prudent person would immediately throw the central electrical breaker at his or her location upon warning.

How should one prepare for such a great calamity? First, expect the absolute worst. One report given to FEMA estimates a grid-down event would result in 90 percent American casualties after one year. I suspect most of these casualties would be the result of dehydration, famine, and disease. Therefore, prepare for these causes of danger in appropriate order: water, food, and then health. Also, in a long-term electrical failure, civil disorder would be a concern.

Keep at least enough water to provide one gallon per day for each person in your family—and keep at least two weeks of water in your home shelter. This should keep you alive through the initial weeks of the crisis. Additionally, you need multiple LifeStraws to filter water, waterBOBs to store water, Katadyn water bottles to filter and carry water, and water purification tablets. Addressing this important survival topic *now* will greatly improve the likelihood of your survival in any extended-length disaster.

The probability of famine after a solar EMP is almost a certainty. It is difficult to ascertain how long a specific individual can live without food, but the consensus seems to be between thirty and sixty days, depending on hydration. With this in mind, I suggest designing your food supply to last for at least sixty days. The sad reality is that the population will dwindle after sixty days—and you might be better able to scavenge for food. Until then, purchase enough freeze-dried food to supplement your normally maintained food inventory. I also recommend keeping a supply of heirloom seeds for gardening after the event.

Contaminated water, weakened immunity, lack of medical care, and missing sanitation all will contribute to increased levels of disease. To combat this, you must have clean water and the training and resources to minimize risk. Keep an adequate supply of N-95 masks, keep multivitamins available, and have antibiotics in your first aid supplies. I also recommend having first aid and medical reference books in your survival materials. Be sanitary to reduce health risks to you and your family or group. Also, bury human waste, wash yourself, and stay away from diseased areas.

A major EMP event could be a civilization-ending disaster. Even a cyberattack against the electrical grid would have some similarities to an EMP event. Journalist Ted Koppel has written an interesting book titled *Lights Out* about the dangers of a grid-down America. His book is more concerned with the grid's vulnerability to a cyberattack, but many of the effects he addresses could also occur with an EMP. Either way, I recommend reading his book. The actions you can take to mitigate the results of this type of occurrence can only be done in advance. Do not wait.

Cyberattack

As we have witnessed over the past several years, cyberattacks on corporations, politicians, and governments are the new frontier of conflict. Motivations behind cyberattacks can range from simple greed and theft to strategic attacks on the military and government. The danger is dire.

Cyberattack objectives can vary from the benign to the catastrophic. In addition, the originating actors can range from a devious child to a sophisticated enemy state. In this book, we are primarily concerned with state or terrorist actors who are intent on widespread destructive actions. Such results can range from the deletion of a bank's depositor records to bringing down the North American electrical grid. In this regard, they are similar to EMP effects.

The greatest systemic risk originates in a grid-down scenario. An enemy attack on the power grid might produce a host of difficulties. For example, we might find it difficult or impossible to locate the source of the attack. This might allow attacks to continue after an initial Pearl Harbor–style attack. A sophisticated attack of this nature could be coordinated with winter weather to increase the death, destruction, and panic caused by the attack. Hackers could cause a cascading power overload that destroys the LPTs and disrupts electrical production for months or years. This would be a low-risk, low-cost method of bringing America to its knees.

How does one prepare for a massive grid-down disaster? The basic rules are the same as preparing for a nuclear war or an EMP. The primary difference is that a grid collapse or a solar EMP does not require a fallout shelter. All other rules apply.

City water systems might not have the ability to operate, and transportation could be impaired. Power would be scarce and dependent on hydro and solar generation—if those control systems were still intact and operable. One of the important considerations in this calculation is to remember that such a large, long-lasting event would impair the government's ability to mitigate the effects. Another concern with a cyberattack is long-term social collapse. As water and food become more scarce, people will become more desperate. In many ways, a significant cyberattack might be the most likely and most destructive man-made event affecting us. It is cheap to produce and difficult to ascertain the source.

If a cyberattack on the electrical grid were designed for maximum destruction, it would probably occur in the middle of winter or at the peak of summer. This timing would increase civilian deaths due to weather and create widespread panic. Some scenarios suggest the middle of winter would create the greatest number of civilian deaths. Therefore, prepare for winter weather in addition to other preparations. Invest in high-quality, low-temperature sleeping bags, warm ski masks, and cold-weather gloves for every family member. If you have a fireplace, keep an adequate supply of firewood. If you do not have a fireplace, consider a "Mr. Buddy" propane heating system for your residence or some other safe system for emergency warmth. I purchased expensive, cold-weather (zero-degree) sleeping bags for this purpose since we do not have a fireplace.

A successful cyberattack on the electrical grid that

caused the grid to collapse would have numerous potential and surprising consequences. For example, transportation could be severely affected. Gas pumps require electricity, and only a few gas stations have backup generators as I previously noted. This also means commercial vehicles would eventually run out of fuel—and so would trucks, trains, and aircraft that transport food, medicine, and other essentials of modern living. If grocery stores only keep one to two days of inventory, and commercial transport can move for one day, then we have two or three days of essential supplies commercially available.

For your preparations for this event, I suggest an emphasis on water-purification techniques, freeze-dried food, lighting, and self-defense. The only area we have not discussed in depth is lighting. Clearly, having an adequate supply of batteries, flashlights, and candles is essential. You may also find old-style lanterns. Just be aware of carbon monoxide issues with flame-based lights and the increased possibility of accidental fires.

Purchase multiple LED flashlights with an extensive supply of replacement batteries, including long-lasting lithium batteries. Periodically test the batteries to make sure they are still charged. Add high-intensity flashlights (tactical lights) for special purposes. Don't forget old-fashioned candles. I recommend Catastrophe Candles, which can be found online or at outdoor shows. Try to avoid scented candles or cheap decorative candles. No electricity means zero light at night, and it will reduce the time you have to be active and productive. Lastly, do not forget a means to light your candles! Have a supply of butane cigarette lighters and an added supply of kitchen matches for your candles and other uses. You might also include waterproof camping matches.

After you have your water supply strategy, your food, your first aid kit, your winter preparations, and your lighting, what else can you do? Another mitigation plan against a cyberattack is to regularly print hard copies of your financial statements and freeze your credit. Banks, insurance companies, and investment firms are frequent cyberattack targets. Protect yourself by having a hard-copy backup of your account balances and freeze your credit to require contacting you before any credit reports are accessed.

Cyberattacks are a significant, high-probability, high-impact risk. Whether the target is your bank or the national grid, the ramifications are substantial. Cyberattacks subject our institutions to daily risk and originate domestically and externally. This is a real high-probability risk. Do not wait to prepare until it is too late!

Civil Collapse

Oddly, as our society becomes more complex, it also becomes more vulnerable to collapse. Joseph Tainter addresses this phenomenon in his book *The Collapse of Complex Societies.* The concept of this trait of complexity is simple in its basic premise. As societies become more complex and interdependent, they also become more vulnerable to a destructive cascading effect if an important element of the society fails. This small failure cascades through the system and magnifies its effect. Think of the 2008 financial crisis and how a series of small events cascaded through the system and nearly destroyed the American financial system.

For our purposes, let's define *civil collapse* as the failure of the central government in Washington, DC. Through a single event (EMP or grid-down event) or a series of events, Washington becomes unable to fulfill its primary purposes of defending the nation, maintaining order, and administering justice. In this scenario, the nation becomes vulnerable to invasion, long-distance war, civil insurrection, and general lawlessness. Some Caribbean nations recently experienced this type of event after Hurricane Irma.

A federal government collapse would likely also cause problems at the state and local levels of government. At the federal level, a collapse might cause difficulties with defense, air travel, payment to federal employees, border control, and public health. However, a collapse of the national government might take time to affect our daily activities. Problems with state and local governments are a more pressing and immediate problem.

The collapse of state and local governments is an immediate concern in the event of a catastrophic disaster. Local police, sheriff's departments, fire departments, and ambulance services are more important to us on a daily basis than most federal services. In this unit, let's concentrate on the ramifications of a collapse of local governments.

Collapse of local governments would guarantee an increase in crimes and fires. If a physically destructive event—a war, an EMP, an earthquake, or something similar—caused the situation, your circumstances could become dire. You must prepare for this possibility by fortifying your residence and having proper supplies, first aid training, and self-defense plans. Proper preparation will allow you to reduce the risk of fire and damage to your home and improve your safety—and still permit you occasional trips away from your residence.

As civil society struggles, expect citizens to form groups to solve or mitigate problems. This is a common reaction to disasters across all societies and cultures. To best benefit in this environment, make yourself valuable. An easy way to increase your value to other people is to pick a skill and educate yourself in that skill. First aid, carpentry, masonry, anything electrical or electronic, ham radio, gardening, and gunsmithing are just a few post-catastrophic disaster skills for short- or long-term survival. In a catastrophic disaster with long-term effects, lower-tech skills are likely to be more immediately valuable than high-tech skills. After all, in a grid-down, freezing, EMP-destroyed world, would you rather have a working fireplace or a fried GPS device?

Even in the best of times, all homes should be fortified! My suggestions in order of importance are:

1. Install dead bolts on all exterior doors and on at least one interior room.
2. Contract for a home security system with audible alarms.
3. Install motion-sensitive security lights with solar backup.

4. Have at least eight-millimeter security film on all exterior windows and glass.
5. Have opaque fences around backyards.
6. Use metal doorjambs for sliding glass doors and doorstops for exterior doors.

These suggestions are bare-bones actions that anyone in any type of residence can choose and pick from in order to make your home more secure. Local government collapse will increase general crime rates and increase the possibility of a home invasion. These simple acts will help protect you and your family.

Fortifying your home also requires reducing the risk of fires. Review the previous section on fires and act accordingly. Remove fire hazards, keep multiple fire extinguishers easily available, and know how to disconnect your gas and utilize your central electrical breaker. In addition, do not forget to install fire and carbon monoxide alarms!

CHAPTER 4

TOOLS

Communications

Being able to communicate during and after a disaster must be a high priority for you. You may need to contact your spouse, relatives, children, emergency responders, or helpful friends. This requires planning.

The basic tool for this need is a cell phone. Cell phones are easily transportable and can contain valuable contact information along with other important information. Keep your phone charged and always have extra chargers in your vehicle and emergency kit. Don't forget to download an app for your local emergency radio station. For Colorado, the Emergency Alert System PEP station is KOA 850 AM. The Federal Emergency Management Agency (FEMA) is adding stations, so check to see if other Colorado stations are active as emergency alert stations.

Also, consider adding a solar battery charger to your cell phone and satellite radio (Sirius XM) to your vehicle. Satellite radio may allow you to receive news updates even if local broadcasters are unavailable.

Cell phones allow two-way communication, but do not ignore traditional radios. You should have a solar- or hand-powered emergency radio in your home and car. Weather radios are perfect for emergencies, reasonably priced, and available with battery, solar, and hand-crank power.

Other communication options include ham radios and Family Radio Service (FRS) walkie-talkies that can be found in any sporting goods store. FRS radios are essentially short-distance, line-of-sight devices that can be useful in your neighborhood. They are easy to operate and do not require a license. Many prudent people decide to address communication plans by acquiring a ham radio license. A ham license allows you to transmit on the FCC-approved amateur radio frequency bands. If you decide to investigate this possibility, check with your local amateur radio club. The entry-level ham license is the tech license, and most clubs offer classes to help you pass the FCC's licensing exam. These clubs tend to include people interested in survival-preparation issues, and many of them are participants in organized emergency communication groups that assist in disasters. During the 2013 floods, these individuals provided emergency contact and support for the public emergency responders. You should be able to purchase a complete ham radio base station for around five hundred dollars.

Be sure your communication plan includes how to stay in touch with your family should you be separated in a crisis. If your cell phone is damaged, do you know your important phone numbers? Write them on a piece of paper now and tape them to your phone! Do you have a meet-up location? Decide on a common location to meet if separated before, during, or after a disaster. The best-laid plans of mice and men may not always work, but it is better to have a plan than to fly by the seat of your pants!

Communication plans are important to your survival and mental well-being in a disaster. At the least, you need a cell phone, but most people should have a cell phone, an emergency weather radio, and satellite radio. Consider acquiring a ham radio and license.

Money

In disaster scenarios, money presents a unique problem. Considering my background as a CFP (Certified Financial Planner), I find this aspect of disaster planning especially interesting. Some of my suggestions are common sense, and some are more apocalyptic.

Basic financial disaster planning centers on temporary survivable events. This means you should plan for and protect your property, which includes having proper insurance coverage. Insure your house, insure your vehicles, and purchase an umbrella liability policy. If you live in a floodplain, buy flood insurance. Your normal homeowner's policy will not cover you if you are in a flood! The first rule of disaster financial planning is to prepare for normal high-probability events. The most common natural disaster in the United States is flooding. Talk to your insurance agent about protecting yourself from losses for events you are more likely to experience— and take photos of everything you own!

Once you are properly insured, you should consider the consequences of more systemic, cataclysmic events. In storms, ATMs may go down. Do you have cash? If ATMs are unavailable, merchants might not be able to accept credit cards, which happened to me when I was traveling in Mobile, Alabama, during a hurricane. All the ATMs were down, and since many gas stations were without electricity, they could not accept credit cards or pump fuel. This experience demonstrates that you should keep a small amount of cash in your vehicle, on your person, and in your home in preparation for such circumstances.

For your vehicle, keep enough cash to pay for at least one full tank of fuel and some convenience store-type food. Obviously, keep the cash hidden but easily accessible. On your person, keep enough cash to satisfy a robber or to purchase supplies or clothes if you are on foot. Evidence suggests some robbers become agitated when victims are unable to give them money, which makes the robber more likely to become violent. Since either situation is likely a temporary event, keeping a large amount of cash is probably not necessary.

Keeping cash in your home is another topic. Clearly, keeping cash in your home presents special issues. In catastrophic disasters, you will likely shelter in place and use your home as a base of operations. Therefore, you would be wise to keep a larger amount of cash than you keep in your vehicle. I suggest at least a two-week supply of cash. By two-week supply, I mean cash to purchase food and water at normal prices to support your family for two weeks. If the event lasts longer than a few weeks, cash might not be an important asset.

In a catastrophic, apocalyptic disaster, an alternate form of money may come into play. Asteroid collisions, Yellowstone erupting, magnetic pole reversal, or nuclear war would likely change the concept of money. In normal times, money is currency that is issued by a central government. In catastrophic times, including war or the collapse of the national government, money is anything of value that will be accepted as a medium of exchange. Diamonds, art, gold and silver, food, water, and ammunition are common historical mediums of exchange. During World War II, some Jewish people and other minority groups used diamonds, art, and gold to help them survive. If you decide to store these alternative forms of money, I recommend an emphasis on food, water, and ammunition. After all, food, water, and ammunition can help you physically survive during a complete collapse, but you cannot eat diamonds, art, or gold!

Gold has an historic place in the experience of surviving catastrophes. For thousands of years, gold had been both money and the backing for money. The exchange value for gold fluctuates just as the value for any commodity changes. However, gold has an allure for people that other commodities do not enjoy. For almost all circumstances, gold is not a reasonable choice to hoard for disasters. In my view, the only exception to this opinion would be if the federal government collapsed. In that situation, paper money would likely quickly lose its value and universal acceptance, and gold would soon resume its former role as money. However, we are talking about a low-probability, high-impact disaster for that circumstance to occur.

If you decide to acquire gold as a hedge against catastrophic disaster, there are several options to consider. You may purchase American legal tender gold coins at any coin shop. I recommend local coin shops of known reputation instead of unknown vendors found online. American bullion coins (Eagles) are available in .1-ounce, .25-ounce, .5-ounce, and one-ounce sizes. Just as with paper currency, try to avoid larger coins since the probability of receiving change in any transaction is unlikely. In an extended emergency, most people are likely to accept gold and silver coins as payment, but you must have a good understanding of the relative value. Since you are considering precious metals for a catastrophic event, avoid foreign gold or foreign silver coins since people might be less likely to accept them.

The second major precious metal option is silver. Silver also has a long history of acceptance as money, and it is much more affordable per ounce than gold. As of the writing of this manual, gold trades at about $1,315 per ounce, but silver is only $17 per ounce. Silver may be purchased as the silver dollar coins many of us knew as children in addition to the new legal tender bullion coins bought at the United States Mint or a local coin shop.

Silver one-ounce coins are purchased individually or in rolls of twenty coins for the "Walking Liberty Eagles." Both the silver and gold coins are beautiful works of art, and many people purchase these coins for disaster insurance, collections, or investing.

Precious metal coins present a storage problem. In large amounts, the coins are heavy and take up a lot of space. You might store them in a safe-deposit box, but in an emergency, you might not be able to access your box. Safe-deposit boxes presented another risk in 1933 when the Roosevelt administration prohibited the private ownership of certain types of gold; banks were required to supervise the withdrawal of these holdings from individually rented deposit boxes. This is unlikely to repeat itself, but it is possible! Home storage of valuable coins also raises similar issues as keeping large amounts of cash: theft or accidental destruction. A partial resolution is to keep precious metals and cash in a fire-resistant home safe. Do not purchase a safe with an electronic lock; in an EMP event, you might not be able to open the safe. Also, contact the insurance agent who is responsible for your homeowner's or renter's insurance. Inexpensive riders to your policy are usually available for these types of valuables in case of theft or fire.

Finally, for the cash or metals you keep in your car and at home, concentrate on small-denomination bills. If you have your emergency cash in hundreds and fifties, you may not be able to exchange them for smaller bills in an emergency—or you might experience paying a hundred-dollar bill for something inexpensive!

Self-Defense

Self-defense is probably the most controversial survival issue. History demonstrates that people bond together to help one another immediately following a disaster. However, there are always exceptions. Additionally, long-term events may result in a collapse of civilized society for a while. In those circumstances, a person must decide how to defend one's self and one's family. After deciding to defend yourself, you must choose whether to use lethal or nonlethal means.

Nonlethal defense should at least offer the possibility of leaving the scene of a problem. Self-defense classes and nonlethal weapons are helpful and readily available. A person might choose a handheld piece of wood similar to a chair leg to keep close to you in your vehicle. Many people use this principle by keeping a baseball bat in their bedrooms. A major drawback to this type of weapon is one must be close to your attacker for it to be effective. Personally, I think you are best served by staying far away from dangerous people! Examples of hand-sized round pieces of prepared wood of varying lengths are found at any improvement store. Expandable batons are also an option, depending on local laws.

My preferred less-than-lethal weapon is a bear spray canister. Bear spray will incapacitate virtually any attacker, and the cans have a respectable range. It is readily available at any sporting goods store for approximately forty dollars. I suggest one can for your car kit and at least one can for your home kit. Be careful with discharging the bear spray so it does not blind you too, do not spray into oncoming wind, and be very careful in enclosed spaces. Also, practice with a can so you understand its proper use.

Lethal weapons present a wide array of choices. Statistically, a handgun is more likely to be useful for self-defense than a long gun. If you are unfamiliar with firearms, please take a shooting class that involves actual time on a firing range. Many police and sheriff's departments offer classes and emphasize proper safety techniques. Also, do not pinch pennies when purchasing a handgun. You want a reliable, safe, high-quality weapon that will protect your life and your family's lives. Your shooting instructor will gladly assist you with this decision. And do not just put it in a safe and forget about it—practice keeps your skills intact.

Besides handguns, long guns are a good addition to your plans in a long-term catastrophic event. Many concerned people emphasize semiautomatic rifles in their survival plans. I question the correctness of that decision. Rifles such as the AR-15 and Mini-14 styles are certainly effective weapons, but they have serious drawbacks. The ammunition is expensive, the firearm is expensive, and significant training is necessary to become effective with these weapons. In addition, such weapons are seldom used in actual self-defense scenarios. Instead of a rifle, I recommend a shotgun.

Shotguns have many advantages and only a few disadvantages. Shotguns are relatively inexpensive, ammunition is inexpensive, and advanced training is not necessary to become proficient. Additionally, shotguns have multiple potential uses. They can be used for self-defense, to hunt for small animals (with proper ammunition), and to hunt for large animals (if using slugs or buckshot). Shotguns are also the only firearm that is reasonably capable of using to hunt birds for food. I recommend purchasing a twelve-gauge shotgun with two interchangeable barrels. The shorter barrel is appropriate for self-defense, and the longer barrel is appropriate for hunting. Store personnel will direct you to appropriate choices, including options that include both barrel styles.

Shotgun selection is also simple. Choose either a Remington 870 or a Mossberg 500. Both weapons have long histories and seldom have mechanical problems. After you purchase your shotgun, buy a shoulder sling and an ammunition sidesaddle. The sling will make carrying your shotgun very easy. A sidesaddle is an accessory to carry additional ammunition on the side of the firearm for easy access. Your new shotgun, combined with a handgun, will likely suffice for any short-term or long-term emergency.

Whether you choose lethal or nonlethal defense, remember that you have a duty to protect your family and yourself. Choose the method that best suits your circumstances and your personal beliefs.

CHAPTER 5

FINAL THOUGHTS

I wrote this manual to assist my fellow Coloradans in preparing to survive a catastrophic disaster along the Front Range of the Rocky Mountains. However, this publication should only be the beginning of your survival planning. Do not procrastinate.

Today, you can purchase enough water and food to meet the minimum requirements for a seventy-two-hour survival emergency. Over the next few weeks, you can assemble your three basic emergency kits for your home, your work, and your vehicle. In the next few months, you can complete first aid training and expand your understanding of the strategies for survival by reading more in-depth books on survival.

You should not delay! We never know when an emergency will arise. A friend of mine used to say, "You never need anything—until you need it." Good luck and remember that it's not if—it's when!

Appendix 1

THE BARE-BONES HOME EMERGENCY KIT

1. One gallon of water per person per day (at least a three-day supply)
2. A three-day supply of food per person for at least three days, at 1,500 calories per person per day
3. LED flashlights and long-life lithium batteries
4. A radio with extra batteries and solar or hand-crank backup features
5. N-95 or N-100 masks for each person (at least a three-day supply)
6. Tools, including pliers, screwdrivers, a mechanical can opener, a hammer, a full-tang knife, and either a small pruning saw or a hacksaw
7. Long-life candles, kitchen matches, and butane cigarette lighters

8. A complete first aid kit for severe injuries
9. An emergency high-decibel hiking whistle
10. Extra-strength garbage bags and a camping toilet with toilet paper
11. Local paper maps
12. A cell phone with multiple types of chargers, including a car charger and a solar charger
13. Emergency space blankets
14. Copies of personal documents
15. Medications and personal care items (soap, toothbrush, toothpaste, etc.)

APPENDIX 2

THE EXPANDED HOME EMERGENCY KIT

1. A multi-tool (including Leatherman and Swiss Army knives)
2. Cash (at least one hundred dollars per family member)
3. Additional food and water to support you for two weeks
4. Clean clothing, especially socks and underwear
5. Wool blankets
6. Games
7. Two-way radios and/or a ham radio
8. Extra car and house keys
9. Work gloves
10. Duct tape and plastic sheets
11. Pet supplies
12. Vitamins

13. Ammunition (if armed)
14. Water purification tablets or LifeStraws
15. A WaterBOB or similar device
16. Airtight plastic food bags

APPENDIX 3

THE HOME FIRST AID KIT

The contents of your first aid kit might vary, depending on the needs of your family and your level of expertise.

1. Adhesive tape
2. Elastic wrap bandages
3. Triangular bandages
4. Nonstick sterile bandages
5. Assorted sizes of roller gauze
6. Band-Aids
7. Butterfly bandages
8. Scissors and tweezers
9. Thermometer
10. Nitrile gloves
11. Petroleum jelly
12. Antibiotic ointment
13. Hand sanitizer

14. Cotton balls
15. Tourniquet
16. Safety pins
17. Emergency dental kit
18. Duct tape
19. Eyewash
20. Antidiarrheal medication
21. Laxatives
22. Antihistamine
23. Aspirin and ibuprofen
24. Cold medications
25. Calamine lotion
26. Hydrocortisone cream
27. Epinephrine auto-injector (if prescribed)
28. Medical history forms for each person
29. Medical consent forms for each person
30. A comprehensive first aid manual

APPENDIX 4

THE EVERYDAY CARRY KIT

Carry this type of kit with you to work, but it could be subject to legal restrictions or work rules in some circumstances.

1. A multi-tool or a Swiss Army knife
2. A paracord style rope
3. A spare car key
4. A small flashlight
5. A tactical pen
6. A cell phone with emergency apps, including Google Maps, a family locator app, a flashlight app, the FEMA app, iHeart Radio, a compass app, the American Red Cross app, and a second first aid app
7. A butane lighter
8. Emergency contact numbers on the back of your cell phone

9. A Breath of Life emergency mask (a must-have if you are in a high-rise building or near airborne toxins)
10. A bandana (for face protection or for emergency first aid)

APPENDIX 5

THE VEHICLE EMERGENCY KIT

1. Jumper cables
2. Road flares
3. Fix-a-Flat
4. Foldable camping shovel and cat litter
5. Auto fire extinguisher
6. Small, empty gas container
7. Matches/butane lighter
8. Adjustable wrench, pliers, screwdriver, knife, multi-tool
9. Hand air-pump and an ice scraper
10. LED flashlight and spare lithium batteries
11. Two space blankets
12. Warm clothing, winter and work gloves, wool blanket, emergency ponchos
13. Duct tape

14. Car cell phone charger and emergency locator beacon
15. Tow strap
16. Water, food bars, LifeStraws

ADDITIONAL RESOURCES FOR PREPAREDNESS EDUCATION

There are many sources for education and training that will assist you in preparing for and responding to major disasters. These are a few of those sources:

Community Emergency Response Teams (CERT)

CERT teams are trained volunteers who have completed a locally taught, national curriculum concerning disaster preparation and response. CERT trains participants in disaster-response skills, including fire safety, light search and rescue, team organization, and disaster medical operations. Even if you choose to not join your local team after completing the training, the information is invaluable—and you will meet similar-minded individuals in your community. CERT is part of Citizen Corps and is coordinated by FEMA and the Department of Homeland Security.

American Red Cross

The Red Cross is an excellent source for disaster-preparation training. The organization offers basic courses in disaster preparedness and tuition classes in first aid, CPR/AED, and wilderness first aid. The wilderness first aid class is especially helpful and strongly recommended. Wilderness first aid is also taught at REI, the Colorado Mountain Club, local recreation centers, JAX, and other independent providers.

Local Hospitals

Your local hospital usually offers education programs on health-related topics, frequently including first aid and specific types of medical issues. Many hospitals offer excellent courses in controlling bleeding caused by an injury.

FEMA Emergency Management Institute

This government facility offers numerous free online courses on a variety of topics. Most courses take two or three hours to complete, and you will be tested on the materials. If you pass the test, they email you a certificate of completion. The well-designed courses are worthwhile.

SKYWARN

The National Weather Service offers its SKYWARN weather-spotter program to trained volunteers. This free program teaches volunteers to identify dangerous weather conditions and explains how to report the information to the NWS.

RACES and ARES

These two services concern emergency communications during disasters. RACES is administered by FEMA, and ARES is coordinated by the American Radio Relay League (AARL). A ham radio license is required to participate. If you have any interest in radio communications, I recommend investigating these services.

Many participants in these programs are interested in disaster preparedness and response.

Coursera

This source for online courses lists multiple free or low-cost courses in disaster preparedness and related topics.

Colleges and Universities

Many academic institutions offer online credit and noncredit courses in emergency management and related issues. These classes are frequently designed for practicing professionals advancing in their careers. An exception is American Military University. AMU offers numerous courses and programs for both professionals and laypersons. For example, they offer an undergraduate certificate in Weapons of Mass Destruction Preparedness.

TEEX

An interesting provider of preparedness education is the Texas A&M Engineering Extension Service. TEEX offers classroom classes in Colorado and also offers online courses. Of particular interest are several classes in cybersecurity.

Books

There are numerous books available concerning general preparedness, EMPs, nuclear weapons, weather, and pandemics. Included in the more comprehensive authors are Arthur T. Bradley, PhD, and Creek Stewart. Stewart is a popular celebrity with shows on the Weather Channel, and he has authored excellent books on emergency kits and emergency vehicles. Dr. Bradley wrote a superior reference book covering most types of catastrophic events and the related survival issues. I heartily recommend both writers and their works.

Printed in the United States
By Bookmasters